KATHLEEN KRULL

ILLUSTRATED BY

DAVID DIAZ

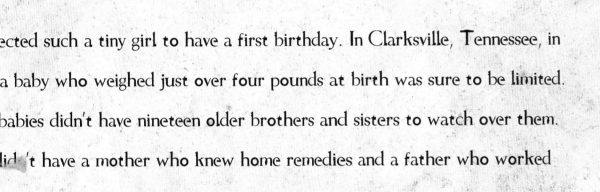

...ected such a tiny girl to have a first birthday. In Clarksville, Tennessee, in ...a baby who weighed just over four pounds at birth was sure to be limited. ...babies didn't have nineteen older brothers and sisters to watch over them. ...did 't have a mother who knew home remedies and a father who worked

...es weren't Wilma Rudolph.

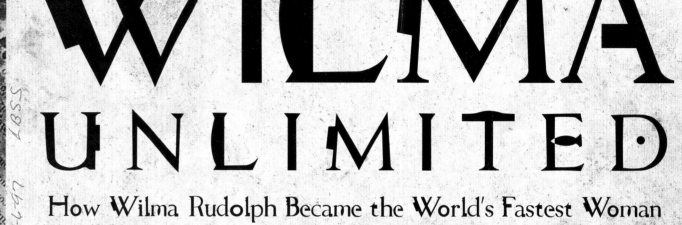

WILMA
UNLIMITED

How Wilma Rudolph Became the World's Fastest Woman

HARCOURT BRACE & COMPANY

San Diego   New York   London

Text copyright © 1996 by Kathleen Krull
Illustrations copyright © 1996 by David Diaz

Requests for permission to make copies of any part of the work should be mailed to: Permissions Department,
Harcourt Brace & Company, 6277 Sea Harbor Drive, Orlando, Florida 32887-6777.

Library of Congress Cataloging-in-Publication Data
Krull, Kathleen.
Wilma unlimited: how Wilma Rudolph became the world's fastest woman/Kathleen Krull;
illustrated by David Diaz.
p. cm.
Summary: A biography of the African American woman who overcame crippling polio as a child to become the first
woman to win three gold medals in track in a single Olympics.
ISBN 0-15-201267-2
1. Rudolph, Wilma, 1940–1994—Juvenile literature. 2. Runners (Sports)—United States—
Biography—Juvenile Literature.
[1. Rudolph, Wilma, 1940–1994. 2. Track-and-field athletes. 3. Afro-Americans—Biography. 4. Women—
Biography.] I. Diaz, David, ill. II. Title.
GV1061.15.R83K78 1996
796.42'092—dc20
[B]   95-32105
First edition
A B C D E

Printed in Singapore

For two strong grandmothers: Margaret Folliard and Agn[...]
—K. K.

For Ariel, my little Buff Man
—D. D.

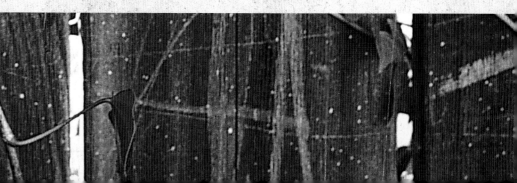

Wilma did celebrate her first birthday, and everyone noticed that as soon as this girl could walk, she ran or jumped instead.

She worried people, though—she was always so small and sickly. If a brother or sister had a cold, she got double pneumonia. If one of them had measles, Wilma got measles, too, plus mumps and chicken pox.

Her mother always nursed her at home. Doctors were a luxury for the Rudolph family, and anyway, only one doctor in Clarksville would treat black people.

Just before Wilma turned five, she got sicker than ever. Her sisters and brothers heaped all the family's blankets on her, trying to keep her warm.

During that sickness, Wilma's left leg twisted inward, and she couldn't move it back. Not even Wilma's mother knew what was wrong.

The doctor came to see her then. Besides scarlet fever, he said, Wilma had also been stricken with polio. In those days, most children who got polio either died or were permanently crippled. There was no cure.

The news spread around Clarksville: Wilma, that lively girl, would never walk again.

But Wilma kept moving any way she could. By hopping on one foot, she could get herself around the house, to the outhouse in the backyard, and even, on Sundays, to church.

Wilma's mother urged her on. Mrs. Rudolph had plenty to do — cooking, cleaning, sewing patterned flour sacks into clothes for her children, now twenty-two in all. Yet twice every week, she and Wilma took the bus to the nearest hospital that would treat black patients, some fifty miles away in Nashville. They rode together in the back, the only place blacks were allowed to sit.

Doctors and nurses at the hospital helped Wilma do exercises to make her paralyzed leg stronger. At home, Wilma practiced them constantly, even when it hurt.

To Wilma, what hurt most was that the local school wouldn't let her attend because she couldn't walk. Tearful and lonely, she watched her brothers and sisters run off to school each day, leaving her behind. Finally, tired of crying all the time, she decided she had to fight back—somehow.

Wilma worked so hard at her exercises that the doctors decided she was ready for a heavy steel brace. With the brace supporting her leg, she didn't have to hop anymore. School was possible at last.

But it wasn't the happy place she had imagined. Her classmates made fun of her brace. During playground games she could only sit on the sidelines, twitchy with impatience. She studied the other kids for hours—memorizing moves, watching the ball zoom through the rim of the bushel basket they used as a hoop.

Wilma fought the sadness by doing more leg exercises. Her family always cheered her on, and Wilma did everything she could to keep them from worrying about her. At times her leg really did seem to be getting stronger. Other times it just hurt.

One Sunday, on her way to church, Wilma felt especially good. She and her family had always found strength in their faith, and church was Wilma's favorite place in the world. Everyone she knew would be there—talking and laughing, praying and singing. It would be just the place to try the bravest thing she had ever done.

She hung back while people filled the old building. Standing alone, the sound of hymns coloring the air, she unbuckled her heavy brace and set it by the church's front door. Taking a deep breath, she moved one foot in front of the other, her knees trembling violently. She took her mind off her knees by concentrating on taking another breath, and then another.

Whispers rippled throughout the gathering: Wilma Rudolph was *walking*. Row by row, heads turned toward her as she walked alone down the aisle. Her large family, all her family's friends, everyone from school—each person stared wide-eyed. The singing never stopped; it seemed to burst right through the walls and into the trees. Finally, Wilma reached a seat in the front and began singing too, her smile triumphant.

Wilma practiced walking as often as she could after that, and when she was twelve years old, she was able to take off the brace for good. She and her mother realized she could get along without it, so one memorable day, they wrapped the hated brace in a box and mailed it back to the hospital.

As soon as Wilma sent that box away, she knew her life was beginning all over again.

FRAGILE